Liv
TO
TELL

A book of truths
and hope
for living again

OLIVIA SAIN

TO
TELL

A book of truths and hope
for living again

www.OliviaSain.com, a division of iBRAND Next Gen, LLC.

ISBN: 978-1-7350998-0-4

Editing: Positively Proofed
                                                    info@PositivelyProofed.com

Design, art direction, and production: Melissa Farr, Back Porch Creative,
                                                    info@backporchcreative.com

Disclaimer: The information provided in this book is designed to give helpful information on the subjects discussed. This book is not meant to be used, nor should it be used, to diagnose or treat any medical condition. For diagnosis or treatment of any medical problem, consult your own physician or professional counselor. The author is not responsible for any specific health needs that may require medical supervision and is not liable for any damages or negative consequences from any treatment, action, application, or preparation, to any person reading or following the information in this book. References are provided for informational purposes only and do not constitute endorsement of any websites or other sources.

Some names and identifying details have been changed to protect the privacy of individuals.

Some lives are lived; others go untold.

Not everyone is lucky enough to live to tell their story.
I'm thankful that I'm able to share my story …
because it means I'm alive.

This book is dedicated to those struggling with an addiction, mental
illness, disease or disability, looking to heal yourself, looking to make
a change, reinventing yourself, repairing yourself to make the most
out of life, searching for hope, searching for reasons to go on, or just
need something to help you get through the day.

This handbook is your personal toolbox. It will teach you the basic
survival skills needed to dig yourself out of a black hole and learn
how to live again. Remember, you've had the tools all along. You just
need to open your toolbox and utilize them.

An orthopaedist repairs bones;
a doctor heals the sick.
Stories have the power to heal the human spirit and broken hearts.

We live in a world that makes it easy to want to escape.

Contents

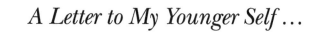

A Letter to My Younger Self …

Dear Olivia,

Brace yourself. You're going to travel to hell and back …
literally!

Your mother experienced four miscarriages before you were
born, so you're a miracle baby. But her initial joy will slowly
turn to anguish as you struggle to overcome obstacles at a
very young age. It's going to be all you know.

You're going to be bullied for having Tourette Syndrome.

You're going to suffer from seizures for 10 years.

You're going to be diagnosed with Central Auditory Processing
Disorder, making traditional settings extremely difficult.

You will enter high school at a fourth-grade reading level.

Oh, did I mention that you will have speech and language
delays?

This is nothing compared to what you're going to face in your
20s. Your 20s will be the worst years of your life.

These experiences will give you life skills you never thought you were capable of. You will be shaped by the good and the bad. One day you'll look back and understand how life events carved the person you are today.

You'll learn to appreciate your struggles because they're a part of the self-discovery process. These uphill battles will shape you, make you work harder, make you humble and, mostly, make you grateful.

Life will again test your mental stability when you lose your father unexpectedly at 23. This will change you forever. You will lose five members of your family in less than five years. You will help take care of them at home in hospice and help administer morphine in their final hours.

You will become an alcoholic because you want to escape the grief and numb the pain.

You will no longer drink for relief, you will drink for survival.

You will fall in love with a heroin addict, who is a girl. She will be the first girl you experiment with; this will make you question your sexuality. She will be the worst thing that ever happens to you.

You will continue to remain in this toxic relationship for eight years. You will endure so much pain while also witnessing loved ones take their final breath.

You will suffer from depression.

You will get kicked out of college.

You will lose hope and be at the end of your rope.

You will become so isolated and wish you could just die. You can't imagine a better life.

And just when you think things are turning around, they take a turn for the worse. At 31, you will enter rehab for alcohol and suicidal thoughts. You will believe the only way out of your misery is your funeral; the only way to happiness is death; the only way for peace is to rest in peace.

You will be diagnosed with bipolar disorder. This will be the hardest diagnosis you've ever had to accept. You will finally understand why you are the way you are. Everything will make sense.

You will not only survive,
you will thrive!

You will graduate from college. You will publish three books. You will begin public speaking after overcoming those speech and language delays.

You and your mom will turn your pain into a purpose by starting a business called Staying Sain. This will provide hope and inspiration despite your heartbreaking losses.

You will start an LGBTQ support group called Butterfly Talks, a group you searched for but couldn't find. This invaluable group will become one of the most successful groups in your hometown.

You will become a motivational speaker based on your experiences and everything you've learned.

You will teach others
how to *live again!*

**This book will teach you
the strategy for
living beyond the pain!**

3 ways of dealing with pain:

1. Being in pain and admitting you're in pain.

2. Being in pain and not doing anything about it.

3. Not knowing you're in pain.

It's not until
YOU'VE
had enough.
It's not until
your behavior
becomes unacceptable
to *YOU* that
YOU

finally **make a change.**

one

The Invisible People

Being invisible means *unable to be seen; not visible to the eye.*

You may not be able to see your mental illness, but you can feel it. You may not be able to see where your addiction is rooted, but you know it's growing somewhere. You may be so isolated that no one can see how lonely you are. You could be in a room full of thousands and still feel like the loneliest person. Your pain may not be visible to the eye, but it is felt in the heart.

That pain was definitely there, but I could not see my addiction or my depression. The painful walls of loneliness and isolation started to break down the moment I reached out to my mom. She could see the pain behind my suicidal thoughts. She would be the one to pull me back onto the road of the living.

It was only a two-hour drive, yet two hours in my mind seemed like forever. What felt like the road to nowhere was what I hoped would be a road to somewhere. Every year, millions upon millions of people are sent down a similar road.

On October 13, 2019, I willingly checked myself into rehab for alcohol abuse and suicidal thoughts. Some do it willingly; others fear it. Some don't have the courage to admit to themselves that they need it. Most people don't want to accept that their lives are "dependent" on a substance that is destructive to their lives. It's very difficult to quit, but it's even harder to maintain.

Could this be the end to my bleeding heart ... or a beginning to a new start?

During the intake process, it was odd watching them go through my belongings. Not to mention, I was never expecting a strip-down search. Talk about feeling violated. It's bad enough having to go to the gynecologist for a yearly pap smear. Well, I'll never again complain about going through the airport's TSA security checkpoint and being randomly chosen for a pat down!

I question why I'm even here and how I got here. It feels like the first day of school. I feel like I don't belong. ***What have I become?*** I'm walking among the living, but no one is watching. I have nothing I want. I can't go home. Why do I have to face this? In the halls, I'm tortured by loneliness. All I do is eat, sleep, and interact with as much normal reality as possible, but that somehow still doesn't help.

After settling in, I can see that the cliques are already formed. These next two weeks are going to go by super slow if I don't make friends. I need to step out of my comfort zone and find someone I can relate to.

One of the first people I met in rehab was Mark. He was a crack addict. He came here with just the clothes on his back after losing everything. Mark asked me a question that is typically asked in prison, *"What are you in for?"* I replied, *"In denial."* Mark laughed. I wasn't sure how I felt about my answer. I felt like I had to admit I did something wrong, but I wasn't sure what it was. Why am I so scared to admit I have a drinking problem when our mutually troubled pasts are what tie us all together?

It's Day 2, and I already called my mom telling her how I don't belong here. Everyone is either court ordered, given ultimatums or has hit rock bottom in other forms. I felt like such an outcast. There's no way

I'll last another day here. Not to mention, we can't listen to music or drink caffeine. Heck, there are more privileges in prison!

Then there's Sara, a heroin addict with two kids. This isn't her first rodeo, just like many of them. She's sick and tired, and tired of being sick. She's hoping to get it right this time. However, I lost all faith when she left against medical authorization, only to be readmitted the same day after relapsing on fentanyl. I knew it was a bad choice for Sara to leave. It's crazy how it takes an outsider to see clearly, but we don't have the same clarity when looking within ourselves.

You ask yourself *how could this even happen*? Well, when you're living with another addict who has been in recovery for 10 years, it almost doesn't take much to trigger them and for them to go back to their old ways. It takes two sick people to be in an unhealthy relationship.

The root cause of addiction is mental illness. The underlying nature of mental illness is self-inflicted, which only prolongs suffering.

It's Day 3. Scott was one of the nicest males I got to know…despite his history of being in prison. He truly was a teddy bear and a perfect example of why you should never judge a book by its cover.

When you're in rehab, you see people for who they truly are. You see their soul, the person they are meant to be. However, life circumstances have completely altered them and sent them on a different trajectory. The outside world only sees them as a junkie, a drug addict or a drunk.

People don't enter rehab because life is good. They enter rehab because they could no longer deal with life on life's terms. They've exhausted all of the options and suggestions they've been offered, and this becomes their last resort.

That's exactly why Alex is sitting next to me. When you lose your mother, brother, sister, and two best friends by the age of 22, you bet your life you're going to be messed up. You wouldn't know that by talking to Alex because he uses sarcasm as a defense mechanism. As I learned more about Alex, I found out he came from a very prominent, wealthy family. He lived in a high-rise condo in a well-known city. He has a significant trust fund that he'll have full access to in the next eight years. He also had access to all of the finer things in life. Even after being court ordered and receiving death threats from drug dealers, the only thing that truly bothered him was how he no longer had access to the finer things in life—something most people never experience.

Even after all of this, he still hadn't learned the lesson of humility. Sometimes it takes something tragic happening before that lesson is learned.

My other rehab friend, Michael, had experienced that tragedy firsthand. His suicide attempt was his wakeup call. He survived, and then he sought treatment. He had not given up.

When you're in rehab, you can't bring much—no sharp objects, no razors, nothing that contains alcohol (including mouthwash). So, I'm not sure how Michael was able to slit his wrist. His family used the Baker Act to get him there. The Florida law enables loved ones to use emergency mental health services to get someone help. His health insurance didn't define substance abuse as a priority. I agree. How can you overcome your addiction when you've lost the will to live? I'll never forget the last words I heard Michael say: "I'm done. I can't take this anymore. There's nothing anyone can say to make me feel better." And he walked out of group. I could see the darkness hovering over him. There was no more hope left in him. He had already checked out mentally. I haven't seen him since.

There are so many unanswered questions about Michael. What's his story? How did he get here? Did everyone give up on him? Did he even have anyone to live for? Or was he just living for himself?

When I was in group, I asked my therapist how often people relapse. I couldn't believe what I heard. **Only 1 in 10 people who enter treatment succeed.** As I looked around my circle, there were only nine of us. This made me question who's going to make it. Will it be none of us? **These aren't just statistics; these are lives.**

As I listened while everyone shared their story, the biggest lesson I learned was that change is possible. People can get better, but only if they truly want to. I learned that people can lose absolutely everything, including their spouse and their children. They can spend time in jail, overdose, be on life support, or end up living on the streets.

Yet, the one thing they never lost was the strength to keep fighting. They were never too scared or broken to create change, and although their faith was tested, they never lost that, either.

These struggling souls walk among us. They're in our family, neighborhood, and at work. We sit beside them every day, but we may not realize what is going on in their brains. Everyone has something they are dealing with, which you wouldn't know just by looking at them. Sometimes we are only a critical thought away from our last chapter.

So how can you help yourself or a loved one
who is struggling with a mental illness or addiction?

How can you help yourself or
a loved one who refuses treatment?

Do you or your loved one think
that their illness defines them?

Are they refusing help because they
wouldn't know who they are without their illness?

The first step to recovery is being honest.
There is no better time to start than now.

A lot of people aren't honest because they don't want to hear cliche responses from those who don't understand. If you're suicidal, you don't want to hear someone tell you, "*Stay.*" What is that going to solve? Do you think it never crossed their mind to stay?

Nice comments don't help. Nice comments won't make them feel better. Nice comments won't save them.

Here's what will help: ***Validate how they're feeling!*** You can't solve their problems, but you can add to their context and help change the way they're approaching it. It's about making them realize that if they choose to ride this out, they will find a solution and redemption. You have to convince them that their feelings of uncertainty will go away. They have tunnel vision that is preventing them from seeing a different outcome.

It's about confiding in the right people.

What's another reason why people aren't honest? It's because stigma still exists. Ignorant people still exist. Those suffering are unwilling to share because they're always thinking that being honest will result in being a burden, being judged, losing what little they have left, like their job.

What's one way to remove stigma?
Talk about it.
Then do something about it.

When I'm asked to give advice, I always think about what advice I would have listened to. After speaking at a summit, one of the questions during the Q&A session was from a father whose children believed their mental illness defined them. They weren't sure who they would be without it. I'd actually never heard this before. I was shocked that anyone would actually want to keep their mental illness.

The more I thought about it, the more I realized I had the same problem, but with grief. I wanted to only feel the bad because that's what I could rely on. It's what I could count on. If I started to feel good, I'd become uncomfortable and resort back to my old ways.

Sometimes the good reminds us of how things don't last forever. If we are used to the bad taking over the good, then we will become reliant on the bad.

You have to believe in yourself again!

Maybe you don't see your place
in life, so you start to doubt
things that don't really matter.
But **YOU** matter.
You matter to **SOMEONE**.
You are loved and **you are WORTHY.**

So, what are you worth?

two

Don't Be a Prisoner to Your Mind

You will never be free until you free yourself from the prison of your own false thoughts.
—PHILIP ARNOLD

Having a prison mentality means being handcuffed to an attitude or a way of thinking. It's like a villain who is trying to keep you believing that there is nothing you can do about it. They want to trap you so you don't have to take time to change yourself. The villain's goal is to attack you like never before. If you accept the villain's mentality, you will never achieve true victory.

I'm a firm believer that the only thing that gets in our way is ourselves. And we stay there by never making a move. I remember the night I couldn't get out of my own way. It was October 10, 2019, and just another dark night. I was alone, drinking, and suicidal. I was standing in my kitchen, gazing at my block of knives, fantasizing about using one on myself. I grew more frustrated with each drink because all I wanted was to leave this world.

**I later realized I didn't REALLY want to die;
I just didn't want to live a bad life.**

I convinced myself that life would never get better and nothing would ever be enough or good enough. I was so consumed by anger, and I hated everything and everyone. I started to see the dysfunction in not only my drinking but in my thinking. Little did I know, I had the devil wrapped around me.

The moment you believe death is your only solution is the moment you become delusional.

**Don't get trapped by the
prison mentality of believing there is
no end to the challenges
you face NOW or will face LATER.**

If we are aware of our own self-sabotage, if we know the right choices to make, then why do we lead ourselves into our own traps? What barriers are keeping us from becoming aware of our intentions and working toward the desired outcome we want to achieve?

I knew exactly what would happen if I drank. I knew it could trigger a bipolar episode. I knew the two are a deadly combination. I knew it would turn me into a person I was ashamed of. But that didn't stop me from drinking. So, why did I continue to be my own worst enemy?

I wasn't ready to let go of the things that made me comfortable. I wasn't ready to grieve over another loss. I believed I was bigger than it. I believed I could find the way to my own salvation. I believed I had all the answers. In reality, the path was much harder and more uncertain than I could ever imagine. Although I was familiar with my traps, I fell for them every time!

You have the power to change; you can quit self-defeating behavior.

If you can identify the ways you self-sabotage, you can start thinking of ways to counteract it. Start looking in different places by:

1. Acknowledging your demons to **OTHERS**.

2. Letting go of the past to make room for new experiences, new relationships, and a new outlook.

3. Allowing yourself to receive the good by eliminating the bad.

4. Removing the bullshit and realizing that life gets better.

5. Letting go of expectations so you can let go of resentment.

We're all prisoners
in the way we conduct our lives.

I want you to imagine being handcuffed behind your back. (If you know what it's like, no judgment. You'll get it!) Being handcuffed can hurt, be slightly painful or worse. You're limited in what you can do. You're constricted, unable to perform daily duties. Uncomfortable, right?

1. How can you live to your full potential if you're restrained?

2. How can you develop an open mind if you're forced into a confined environment?

3. How can you receive help if you are forced into isolation?

31

What are you handcuffed to?

That old story?

That old relationship?

That old way of thinking?

That old habit?

Guilt?

The past?

What others think of you?

An addiction?

A mental illness?

A job?

A financial rut?

A diagnosis?

What are you still holding onto
that's keeping you a prisoner to your past?

Everyone has a fighting spirit, even if you can't see it. Reminding yourself that it's not over and there's still time to get out is to your advantage. It's not the uniform you wear; it's the gear you have within yourself that will get you through. **Set yourself free by unleashing yourself.** You had the key all along, you just needed to learn how to use it.

Who's protecting *you* from *you*?

3 Things I'm a Prisoner to...

1.

2.

3.

Feelings Do Not Define Your Destiny

Feelings are like waves.
We may not be able to stop them from coming,
but we can choose how we ride them.

When I first started writing this book, my therapist said, *"You can't write this book until you are healed."* Well, I disagree, and here's why. Once we cross over to the healing side, some of that pain can fade away. As time goes on, it becomes easier to forget how we were feeling. **I never want to forget the pain and the struggles I went through.** It's a raw, awful reminder of a dark time. I want to be able to catch myself and have my safety net anchored so I'll never revisit that place again.

Living with mental illness and addiction is frustrating. It's lonely, it's discouraging, and it's damaging. You feel crappy for days, weeks, months, and even years.

At times, it's hard to distinguish feelings from fear. I remember telling myself that life would never be enough. I was always searching for something more, but I couldn't put my finger on it. I wanted to feel a certain way, a feeling that I would recognize once I felt it. But, even then, would it be enough? Will anything ever be enough?

I started to believe everything I told myself. If I'm thinking it, then it must be true! I became delusional and paranoid.

I didn't want to live the rest of my life this way. I can't expect every moment to be a high. It's okay to have mediocre moments. If I expect everything to be perfect, I'm setting myself up for disappointment. It's up to me to capture these moments and stop them. Otherwise, I won't accomplish anything with this way of thinking.

Don't make decisions based on a temporary feeling. Your current situation IS NOT permanent.

The moment we believe our feelings are a prediction of the future is the moment we become delusional. False feelings can alter our brain and influence our thoughts, choices, and outlook. Our thoughts begin to control our destiny. When feelings take over, we lose our grip on reality.

False feelings come from a wound that hasn't healed.

We may not be able
to stop thoughts
from coming,
but we can *choose*
where they take us.

Reject, don't react—This is the first step in opening up your mind and being able to recognize where these feelings are coming from. When you're honest with yourself and your loved ones, they can help you think rationally through what you're going through.

We only allow what we *tell others*.

Don't forget the pain and struggles you went through.

Keeping that feeling just below the surface is a reminder of where you've been and how you never want to return.

It's normal to go there; it's *not* normal to stay there.

four

Own Your Authentic Self

When we're not living as our authentic self,
we fall down,
we lose a sense of who we are,
and we forget the beauty in our story.

When I was in rehab, a neurologist gave a lecture about how addiction affects the brain and why we become addicted. One of the most fascinating lessons was about how it's not about how much you drink, it's how that drink affects your core values, your control, and how you react.

It's like the "before" and "after" effect. What were your values before your addiction? What were your values during addiction? Keep in mind, quantity is irrelevant to addiction. The desire to ingest or inject something you know is killing you is when your core values become conflicted. Instead of changing our addiction, we change our core values for our addiction.

As humans, we are addicted to what we don't have. We spend our whole lives trying to attain what we *think* will fulfill us, what we *think* will be enough. We quickly forget that what we *have* is enough, that *we're* enough. The only thing we need to achieve is *self-acceptance*.

Humans are like packages: We're all trying to reach our destination. Some arrive on time, some arrive late, some get lost, others never arrive. Then there are the fragile packages. They are only one drop away from shattering. By the time they reach their landing place, they arrive in a vastly different condition than when they started. They, like us, may not be in the best condition to function.

If you rush the process, you could do more damage to yourself.

We all take different paths to reach our destination. Some take detours, some hit dead ends, some have an easy journey, and others are left behind.

To those who are arriving later, perhaps it's not your time yet. You may have all the potential in the world, but maybe you are not where you're supposed to be. **We all belong somewhere; the journey is all about finding our place in this world.**

There is no such thing as same-day delivery in life. As Abraham Lincoln once said, *"Good things come to those who wait, but only what's left from those who hustle!"*

Life is not a race. Go at your own pace.

Races are timed; life is not. The only timeline is what we give ourselves while comparing ourselves to others. Remember, you don't have to be first to the finish line; you just have to cross over it.

At times our authentic self gets buried deep inside us, like an avalanche tumbling down. So many things build up in our life, and it pushes down on us when we put away our authentic self.

Finding a way to dig yourself out is the moment you *preserve the real you.* **It's the moment your inner core is saved.**

Take your power back by releasing a burden.

One of the biggest burdens I carried around was being gay. After the loss of my father, I gave myself permission to do things I probably never would have done if he were still alive. My father kept me grounded and accountable. There was an expectation I had to meet and a persona I believed I had to keep up.

I struggled with the complexity of my sexuality. *Can I change this? Can I fix this? Can I ignore this?* My sexuality isn't something I can put in a box and leave for later. It stays with me wherever I go.

When I came out, I thought I was going to be released from this burden, free to be myself. I thought I was going to be released from everything that kept me in a black hole. I was wrong.

It did not fix how I looked at myself. It did not fix what I thought my father would think of me. Would he have supported me? Would he be proud? I struggled with these uncertainties.

Society is more accepting of straight lifestyles. However, just because something is comfortable doesn't mean it's healthy.

Although I experienced more conflict by being my true self, I finally found happiness. I found freedom. **I had to force myself to reach out of my comfort zone and become uncomfortable.** Doing so was the only way to overcome my fears.

Being honest with yourself and others is the only way to be released from your burdens. Loving yourself and loving others is a big part of how people cope with difficult challenges in life. If you love yourself, then you let people love you back. That's what being authentic is.

Being your authentic self means *being at home in your own skin.* If you are a shallow version of yourself, you'll be eternally miserable.

Becoming aware of your authentic self starts with listening to the right voices. We all have good and bad voices that become our source of direction. If you become conflicted, consider confiding in someone you trust who can help you be sure you are making the right decisions. Every decision we make involves both positive and negative energy. Keep in mind the balance you desire.

3 Ways I Can Start Owning My Authentic Self...

1.

2.

3.

Become an
unmasked version
of yourself.

Are you masking who you truly are?

Is it possible to get through today without masking?

What does self-acceptance look like?

Emotional masking means hiding the fragile parts of ourselves from others, the world, the truth, and our own story. We fear we will be a burden, people won't understand, we won't be taken seriously, we'll be judged. The list is endless.

We can mask any problem from the inside out, but it distorts our relationship with our bodies. **Masking creates an identity that we constantly struggle to maintain.** Emotional masking comes with "problems." Even if it's not physically harming us, it leaves behind a lot of guilt, shame, self-doubt, and isolation.

I know what it's like to mask an addiction, a mental illness, a feeling. I officially crossed over to the dark side. I didn't want to hear the typical cliche responses. I didn't want to hear "it will get better," "you have your whole life ahead of you," "suck it up," etc.

People don't want to be told to stay strong. They want to be inspired to open up. They need to be given reasons to be vulnerable. They need to know that when they open up, there will be a resolution, not an execution.

One of my favorite movies growing up was *Star Wars*. My father and I bonded over this movie. One of the most iconic villains is Darth Vader. He's not only known as a villain enemy, but he is known for concealing his true identity.

Like Darth Vader, we're all wearing different masks to cover up our feelings, fears, emotions, struggles, and pain.

When you keep your struggles silent, you only hurt yourself. Help yourself by letting others help you.

When you mask
your feelings,
you rob yourself of
your authentic self.
You are creating
emotional starvation.

3 Ways I Mask My Feelings...

1.

2.

3.

five

S.O.S.
(Save One's Self)

*Don't endorse the things
that are hurting you.*

We all have that defining moment when we have to choose to either sink or swim. You reach that defining moment when you've had enough, when you have no more fight left in you. The moment you finally find the courage to walk away from that toxic relationship, the moment you admit you are addicted to something, the moment you ask for help, the moment you choose to surrender to change, the moment you just can't do it anymore. When you begin saving yourself, you make the choice to depend solely on yourself.

I was drowning in a relationship with a drug addict for eight years. If you've loved an addict, you'll understand. If you've never loved an addict, you're lucky.

Loving an addict was one of the hardest experiences I went through. Knowing when to let go was even harder. Between the sleepless nights, the constant worrying, the endless efforts of trying to save her, without even realizing it, I became co-dependent. I sacrificed my own well-being for someone else. I spent so much time trying to fix her that I forgot what it felt like to think for myself.

Never sacrifice your own well-being for another person.

I don't know what it's like to be a drug addict, but I do know what it's like to love one. At times, I believed it was harder for me because I was the sober one. I could remember everything and feel everything, and she would have no recollection of the things that still haunt me.

I was so afraid of grieving over her because I had already lost so many loved ones. I tried so hard to hold onto her. I later realized I was always grieving over her. There's no greater pain than watching someone you love who loves their drugs more than they love you.

We reach a point where we ask ourselves, *"When is enough enough?"* Sometimes it takes something so bad to happen that we finally make a move. How can we save others when we only have one life preserver?

You know you've made the right choice when the pain of leaving outweighs the pain of staying. As we grow older and wiser, we no longer tolerate the things we used to. Our past helps us discover our best present. You must think about your own health and well-being. If not, others will take you down with them.

If you stay in a black hole, you'll only get deeper, and it will become harder to climb out. It's like quicksand: Unless someone throws us a rope, we can't make it out alone.

Don't go back to what you worked so hard to let go of and get rid of!

Saving yourself means loving yourself. Loving yourself means...

Having enough respect to know what you deserve.

Freeing yourself from anything that may be harmful to you.

ALWAYS making yourself a priority.

Choosing better relationships moving forward.

Freeing yourself from any constraints, experiences or circumstances that might hinder you from achieving your goals.

We all have that ace up our sleeve, reserved knowledge or information that saves us from our situation. We all have that secret weapon, a secret power we hold within that gets us through.

Take care of yourself. That is your most important asset. There are plenty of excuses you can tell yourself, but each one is an excuse to not be good to yourself.

You should make decisions for yourself — not others.

3 Things I Need to Let Go...

1.

2.

3.

3 People I Need to Let Go...

1.

2.

3.

six

If You Want to Change Your Life ... Prove It!

If you are able to go from obstacle to opportunity,
that is when you transform your life.

I couldn't wait until 5 p.m. so I could start drinking. That's when the creative juices started flowing. That's when I'd be on that high and anything was possible. That's when the ideas and opportunities seemed endless to me.

On the other end of the sword, that's when the suicidal thoughts kicked in. That's when the depression would take over. That's when isolation became my only friend. I knew drinking was making my thoughts worse, but I continued to drink. I knew I was getting deeper in my addiction, but I didn't care. I knew all of these things were bad for me, but it wasn't enough for me to change. As miserable as I became, I remained the same until I hit rock bottom. Hitting rock bottom is different for everyone. Mine was the moment I wrote a suicide note to my loved ones.

What was the answer to ending my suffering? How did I bounce back? When did the mask finally come off? It was the moment I told my mother I was suicidal. That was the moment of relief. Although my burden was finally released, I still had to confront my demons.

I believe we do the same thing over and over and expect the **same** results!

To be the change in your life, you need to first decide to be the one to make it happen. Change requires not just waking up but changing how you think. It requires a conscious effort to make the conscious decision to change.

Why do we continue to live in the same patterns?

Why do we feel powerless and incapable of making positive changes?

Can we begin to let go of habitual thinking, the constant negative results of our actions, and learn to accept and change into a better version of ourselves?

What actions can we take?

What is available to us to begin changing our patterns?

We all have tendencies toward addictive behavior. What are we capable of doing to let go of that pattern, to become the true version of ourselves?

What does it mean to "*do* better" instead of "*getting* better"? What does it mean to practice "letting go" instead of "releasing"?

I know what you're thinking. *How do I answer these tough questions? Where do I even begin?* They might make you feel bad about yourself, your past or the choices you've made. Realistically, they are meant to help you think more clearly about your future instead of harp on your past. As I asked in Chapter Two, *What are you handcuffed to that keeps you a prisoner to your past?*

We all put up barriers that keep us from change, a new way of thinking, even a new way of living. I believe we live in the same patterns because we are afraid of where we've been and where we will end up. Patterns are comfortable and predictable.

As I wrote this part of my book, I really had to stop and think back to all that I've been through. What choices (positive and negative) have I made that determined where I am now? How and when did I become a better version of myself?

I could never understand why I kept making the same bad choices over and over, even when I knew better. If I'm aware of my choices and their consequences, then why do I keep repeating the same behavior? The answer is simple. I was always in the same place mentally, looking for the same thing.

Relationships are a perfect example. Do you ever wonder why you keep attracting the same kinds of people? Again, it's because we're in the same place, looking for the same thing.

A lot of our unease comes from the fear of repeating the same mistakes and going back to our old ways.

Unfortunately, what we have done to ourselves has led us to this point. Our habits have become a part of us, and what we do daily affects how we perceive the world. This affects how we interact with others, the actions we take, and the stress we feel every day.

Knowing the right action and knowing the right way to choose that action is critical, and it is ultimately up to you. Most of us don't listen to our inner voice. We either choose to live in the pattern we are in, or we choose to ignore the destructive energy in our lives. Before we can make any real change in our lives, we must become aware of it. Loss of control and being powerless keeps us addicted to our old ways and gives us no outlet to change. We no longer let ourselves do what our thoughts tell us to do.

Before you consider a change, understand that the steps in this process are not a one-size-fits-all. One of the reasons I dislike treatment centers so much is because they treat everyone the same. It's like giving everyone the same antidepressant and expecting the same results. Mental illness and addiction are much more complex than that. Recovery should be tailored to the individual, not the problem. This applies to all problems, because we are all recovering from something.

We must detach ourselves from patterns of compulsion. This is why we need to be focused on the inner landscape of ourselves, which can only improve through awareness. We need to realize our true self resides deep within our subconscious.

The past serves as a reminder of the poor decisions we've made, the wasted potential, the emotional hurt, the failures, the yearning for success, and the overwhelming anxiety of living one's life to the fullest. The past can help us understand what has led us to where we are now. In order to surrender to change, we must look at the present to help us make needed decisions.

Surrendering means being humble enough to admit we need help. It's about being content even though we're not sure where that may lead.

If you're reading this book, something isn't working in your life. Or maybe you're reading this for a loved one who needs help.

These questions will help you or your loved one know if they're truly ready to change:

1. *Do you believe that you deserve to live a changed life?*

2. *Do you believe that you are worthy of receiving help?*

3. *Are you willing to surrender to change?*

If you answered NO to any of these questions, you need to change what you believe about yourself and what you think you know. Your beliefs come down to your own defiance. For instance, refusing to acknowledge that you need help; refusing to recognize signs of your partner's infidelity; or refusing to admit that what you're doing is bad for your health. All of these road blocks will keep you from moving forward.

If you talk yourself out of everything, then everything will stay the same.

Emotional pain keeps us from moving forward. It's like a bad wound in the brain. You can't see it, you can't pinpoint it, but it does exist.

Recovering is about moving past the past, making a new future, and doing things differently. **You are powerful enough to change your life.**

So, fight for the life you hope to rewrite.

Making changes will take immense effort, and you will need to be open to experimenting and facing new challenges. Start every day with an open mind. When you let go of your pride, you can get a better grip on life. It is possible to create change even without your ego becoming the enemy.

We don't have to know our pathway, we just have to know our next step.

If you want to change your life, follow these 3 steps...

1. See It.

Visually see the problem. Recognize that there is a problem. Examine your habits and pinpoint the root of the problem.

2. Know It.

Simply bring the attitude of self-awareness and know that something needs to change. We can still know something but choose to do nothing about it.

3. Confront It.

It's not until we challenge our compulsions, ask for help, and take action that we can start to free ourselves.

3 Things I Want to Change in My Life...

1.

2.

3.

seven

Act It
Until You Become It

The well that you drink from is the well that you think from,
and will eventually be the well that you become.
What well do you drink from?
— SIMON T. BAILEY

If you've learned anything from the saying "fake it until you make it," you might try to imitate someone else. You might try to look like them, behave like them, or act like them, but you won't succeed. How can you fake something you don't believe in? In order to make something truly incredible, we must first believe in it, then make it a reality. You must act it before you become it.

In rehab, we did an activity where 30 sheets of paper were laid out in five rows. One by one, we had to step on pieces of paper by guessing how to get through. The therapist would buzz us if we stepped on the wrong paper. With each misstep, we'd have to start all over. Everyone in the group had to make it through. It was a fun activity because we were able to memorize the path and get closer to the end.

What was the point of this activity? What did this represent? **It's okay to start over!**

In starting over, you'll know what to do because you've already put in the legwork. We watched as others went through the same exercise. By watching them, we were able to see the way more clearly. This allowed us to see others take a wrong step and taught us what not to do when it was our turn. Just as in this paper-trail exercise, we all take different paths to recovery, but we're all trying to get to the same destination.

Rehab reinforced self-discipline and maintaining a schedule. It taught me how to prioritize my day. I was used to waking up and immediately checking my phone, my emails, and social media, which had become my daily ritual—so much so that I was addicted and experienced anxiety without it. Rehab forced me to be on someone else's schedule and live by their rules. I had no choice but to wake up to no technology and no music, and to grab my decaf coffee, eat breakfast, and learn how to be content with the little things in life.

So, what will *YOU* do differently?

Once you begin to alter your way of thinking, your mind starts to adapt to a new way of learning. Eventually you will understand the thoughts and ideas that drive your subconscious mind. This is the mind's way of improving itself. As you practice, you can keep learning. As you train your mind, it will become better and better at coping with life.

The practice is not simple. Your issues must be worked out. Like peeling an onion, you must pull back each layer in order to uncover the core issues you face. Yes, there will be tears involved—just like peeling that onion—but as you expose each underlying issue, you'll eventually get to the best part: that moment of relief and, ultimately, healing. If you don't get down past all of the layers, then no matter how hard you try, you will never make it.

No matter how good you are, there will always be obstacles you must overcome.

It seems so simple, yet we rarely (if ever) believe in our own potential for success. Potential is like a flower; to blossom, you must water it. What are you watering your potential with? With each move, we must believe in ourselves so we can perform the next move. As we perform our movements, we believe in our own potential to be beautiful and successful. But first we must remove the old pattern of "bad play" from our game.

We don't realize our potential until we exceed our expectations.

What you do every day will determine if you stay or walk away.

In order to become the person you want to be, focus on changing just one thing each day. Don't overthink it. Don't make it more complicated than it has to be. Do one thing differently. Whether that means foregoing that glass of wine after work, swapping sweets for a workout at the gym or replacing negative self-talk with self-love, get creative!

The Power of *Influence*

Fuel your body with crap and you'll feel like crap. That old saying, "*You are what you eat,*" is so true.

Our moods and our minds are no different. **We are greatly influenced by whom we surround ourselves with, whom we choose to turn to, and whom we rely on.** Whom we talk to daily determines who we are. Just like circumstances can prevent us from reaching our fullest potential, so can people.

People can either make us or break us. They can impact our emotions, thoughts, and choices. If you're in a dark place and surrounded by depressed people, then you're going to become more depressed.

Take a deeper look and consider who you want to attract in your life. **Surround yourself with people who motivate you, not dominate you.**

Then ask yourself:

> *Who can throw you a rope?*

> *Who can reel you back in?*

3 Ways I Can Become 'It'...

1.

2.

3.

eight

Trust in the Universe

You can't connect the dots looking forward,
you can only connect the dots looking backward.
So you have to trust that the dots will somehow connect in your future.
You have to trust in something—
your gut, destiny, karma, whatever.
— STEVE JOBS

My father used to wear a cross necklace every day. For years, he gave the cross necklace to my sister when he traveled on business. He'd tell her to hold onto it until he got back. Unfortunately, my father lost the cross necklace and replaced it with a St. Christopher necklace, which he wore every day until the day he died.

After my father passed away, we collected his belongings, including his St. Christopher necklace. My sister and I looked at each other and said, "Who gets the chain and who gets the charm?" We didn't want to split the necklace, so we decided to talk about it later.

That same week, my mother went to the cleaners to pick up my father's black suit, which we needed for his funeral. Whenever the cleaners find personal belongings in the pockets, they give it to you in a paper bag. My mom opened the paper bag and she couldn't believe what she saw: the original cross necklace my dad lost. Now my sister and I didn't have to split the necklace after all.

We were each given the necklace that meant the most to us. My sister got the necklace my father would give to her as a child and I got the necklace my father wore when he passed. This was the first moment in my life when I truly believed in a higher power. I would often ask for signs but never got a response. To my surprise, the answer to my pleas was shown to me in this most meaningful way. I now believe that there is so much more to this earth than what we can see.

Sometimes life doesn't seem to be in our hands. We start to reach for something else, something outside of ourselves, something greater than the mind, a spiritual act that turns fear into awe.

When the world around us seems to be collapsing, we can find ourselves questioning everything. Our search for answers and understanding allows us to look beyond our doubts, questions, fears, and insecurities. We can then start looking at things from a new perspective.

When I was in the depths of my depression, I was unhappy, angry, resentful, and miserable. **I needed something greater than myself to help me out of my own misery.**

That "higher power" can be anything you want it to be. It can be spirituality, faith, GOD, a deceased loved one, a program, a treatment center, even yourself—whatever gives you the power to believe that there is more to life. It should be what works for you, not what works for other people, something that gives you peace and hope as you navigate all the things in this world that can't be explained.

Sometimes we don't experience or appreciate a spiritual awakening until we lose something. The only thing worse than losing something we love is losing ourselves along the way.

Faith **doesn't necessarily teach us how to cope, but it can give us** *hope.*

Hopelessness is just a visitor.

We don't always see that our most meaningful adventures take place in the face of hopelessness.

Everything we experience is created by design.
We come out on the other side with
armor and power,
helping us find inner strength in the
face of hopelessness.

Imagine you're in a dark room with no electricity. You can't see. You have to rely on your other senses to find the exit. You're grasping to find the smallest twinkle of light that shines between the cracks. That little glimmer will help guide you out. It's not until you get to the opening and step through that door that you begin to see the light and join the living.

Don't allow circumstances to change you. Instead, change the circumstances.

There are so many things that affect us externally, but when things hit us internally, we choose how we process circumstances. I'm a firm believer that hope is our saving grace in times of despair. Without hope, we have nothing to hold onto.

Hope isn't something we wake up with. It's not an instinct like eating or sleeping. It's a daily practice. *In order for hope to work during desperate times, we must implement it in our daily life.*

We hope we can get through the days, and the days don't have to be as scary as they once were. Hope can help us grow stronger during troubling times and give us strength we maybe didn't know we had.

How do you live in hope through your daily life?

By identifying one thing we have that we value and appreciate, we can begin to live out the hope that exists inside of us. It's important to be deliberate in these practices.

Begin each day by incorporating hope into your vocabulary. Instead of telling yourself, "My life is never going to change" or "I'm never going to get better," tell yourself, "I hope my life will get better, I hope I will get better." Change "won't" to "hope." It sounds simple, but it's all about perspective.

The struggle must never overcome you.

When I was In rehab, I was told a story called *Potatoes, Eggs & Coffee Beans*. It was about a father showing his daughter how potatoes, eggs, and coffee beans react differently once they're dropped in boiling water. As he dropped in the potatoes, eggs, and coffee beans one by one, the daughter could see how each one changed. Ultimately, the potato became soft, the egg became soft, and the coffee beans produced a rich aroma that brought a smile to the daughter's face.

The moral of the story is how we all face adversity in life. Each of us reacts differently. The coffee bean changed after being exposed to boiling water, but it turned into something new and better. *When life throws you curveballs, are you a potato, an egg, or a coffee bean?*

What you believe and what you tell yourself determines how you move forward.

3 Things That Give Me Hope...

1.

2.

3.

It's hard to see the light at the end of the tunnel when you're in a dark place.

Once we find the power of perspective, it starts to manifest in our lives.

We are the creators of our own destiny, but sometimes we need something to help lead us. Otherwise, we'll lead ourselves right off a cliff. **Find something greater than yourself to help guide you and keep you on track.**

3 Ways I Can Trust in the Universe...

1.

2.

3.

nine

Inspiring Words for Those Who Want to Give Up

Don't give up before the miracle happens.

A commencement speech, written for graduates who are about to set sail and take on the world, offers words of wisdom and inspiration. These traditional speeches only come along once or twice in a lifetime. That's unfortunate, really. Who couldn't use some insight and a pep talk more often?

With that in mind, I offer this commencement speech for those who have yet to make it to the finish line:

> We're all looking for an escape from reality. It may seem easier to give up when you're feeling powerless, defeated or

broken. When you believe there are no good choices, you can't possibly envision any solution. We're all searching for inspiration to keep fighting.

I know what it feels like to give up. But I also know what it feels like to never give up. There are things that happen in life that cause us to be permanently scared of what lies ahead, scared of the unknown. Sometimes not knowing is best because it protects us from worrying before we need to. It keeps us from losing our minds.

Thomas Edison once said, **"Our greatest weakness lies in giving up. The most certain way to succeed is to try just one more time."**

My greatest failure was being dismissed from college. At the time, I was not mentally up for the challenge. On top of everything else that happened in my life, the stress of giving up on my college dream was the straw that broke the camel's back. I didn't know how I was going to come back from that. It was the final disappointment. I was no longer at a standstill; I was in a black hole.

My father always taught me to have a Plan B in case Plan A didn't work out. Since college was no longer an option, I became a hotel barback/bartender. I figured I could work my way up the hospitality ladder. I quickly realized how unhealthy the environment was for my mental and physical health.

Already struggling with alcohol, I couldn't have chosen a worse environment. It was like getting free candy. Between the long hours and hard labor, I asked myself, "Is this worth it?"

But my Plan B yielded once again to my Plan A. After a long, hard road of working to reach reinstatement, I was accepted back into college. Unfortunately, I had to start from square one because the catalog had changed. This was another moment that tested my will to keep going.

I'm proud to say on December 15, 2017, I walked across the stage and accepted my diploma. Looking back, it would have been a lot easier to request a medical leave from college. However, would I have worked just as hard? I finally understood the importance of my education, and I have a greater appreciation for it.

By keeping my vision and never giving up on my goals, I finally made it to the finish line. As I walked on stage to accept my diploma and hear my name being called, it meant so much more than anyone could ever realize.

Graduation has a different meaning for everyone as they receive their diploma. For some, it's an easy accomplishment. For me, it sometimes seemed unattainable. Now, it's an accomplishment that will open new doors and give me opportunities not otherwise possible.

In an auditorium full of thousands, I realized I didn't just graduate from college, I graduated from my obstacles.

In order to never give up, you must believe that something greater is waiting for you. You must believe in something worth living for. You must believe that you are a vital part of something and that you will not just endure the worst of times, but you will be able to carry on.

Sometimes we don't see the value in our struggles until we experience that hardship. Sometimes it takes failure to learn what's important in life. When you stop using the tools necessary to push ahead, you stop short of the miracle.

3 Ways I Can Not Give Up ...

1.

2.

3.

ten

Live Again

We're all searching for a deeper meaning of existence,
a new perspective, a new way of doing things.

We're not creating a life we desire when we're just existing. For the longest time, that's exactly what I was doing. My main goal was merely getting through the day. At night, once my head hit the pillow, there was a sigh of relief that I had one more day behind me. I survived. Before long, panic would set in and I would start thinking, *"How am I going to get through tomorrow?"*

There were days I was gasping for air, anxiety consumed my every thought, and there was no passageway for joy to seep in.

I became distressed and haunted by bad memories and experiences. This stole my joy and convinced me that life would never be as good or good enough. I became trapped by my past, miserable in the present, and hopeless for the future.

We should be able to wake up and greet each day as a new adventure and excited about the opportunities ahead. It's hard to feel the warmth of the sun and see the brightness of the day when you're drowning in quicksand. It takes everything in you to not suffocate.

Everyone has a different perspective about what it means to live. Yet it takes constant effort to maintain a healthy outlook. We're not always happy, but we have happy moments.

Making yourself feel good starts with awakening your senses. You have to start by taking care of your physical, mental, and emotional health. This is the only way to repair yourself and make the most of your life. Without that needed healing, there is no well being.

"We repeat what we don't repair."

—CHRISTINE LANGLEY-OBAUGH

Sometimes we need an alternative path to take control of our life. The first step is by taking personal inventory of where you are. Then think about the best times in your life:

1. Where were you?

2. What were you doing?

3. Who were you with?

4. How did they make you feel?

Then think about the present:

1. Where are you now?

2. What's missing?

3. What needs to change?

On my 30th birthday, I asked my friends and family to write me a eulogy. I'm sure you're thinking, "*That's morbid and why would you want that?*" Well, I learned a very profound lesson after losing my father. As I heard all the great stories and positive things people had to say, I asked myself, "*Why do we wait until someone is gone to tell them how important they were and how much they meant to us?*" We immediately think of all the things that went unsaid.

I wanted everyone to imagine I was really gone and as if they would never see me again. What had they wished they'd said? What would the world be like without me? Have I impacted their life? Have I taught them any lessons?

This wasn't meant to be self-serving; it was meant to change perspectives and prompt everyone to take inventory of how they're living their life.

Instead of thinking about the big picture, we spend too much time worrying, living in fear, and consumed with ourselves. It's not until something happens that we start to think about the life we really want to live.

We ask ourselves:

1. *Do I always play it safe?*

2. *Are my beliefs aligned with how I'm living?*

3. *If I died today, would I be happy with the life I lived?*

4. *Did I live life to its fullest?*

5. *Was there something I always wanted to do but never got the chance?*

6. *Were there things in my life that I could have done differently?*

7. *Do I have any regrets? If so, can I still make amends?*

8. *What do I want to create?*

9. *How do I want to see my life replayed when my time is up?*

10. *How do I want to be remembered?*

So, what does it mean to live again?

To live is to *move forward.*

To live is to *let go.*

To live is *stop self-defeating behavior.*

To live is to *save one's self.*

To live is to *always have something to look forward to.*

To live is to *wake up and be excited about the day.*

To live is to *look beyond the hour.*

To live is to *experience joy again.*

To live is to *choose happiness.*

To live again means to *be released from your past.*

To live again means to *live beyond the pain.*

To live means to *enjoy the sand between your toes with the warm sun beating against your skin and listening to the calming sea.*

To live again means *leading a life you don't have to escape.*

To live again means *having a life worth living instead of just getting by.*

To live again means *putting the pieces back together so you're better than ever.*

To live again means *living beyond your disease, disability or tragedy.*

To live means to ***embrace the life you're meant to live!***

To live is not only what people say about you when you leave the room, it's what they say about you when you leave this world.

3 Ways I Can Start Living Again...

1.

2.

3.

About the Author

Olivia Sain is a therapeutic storyteller, speaker, and author. Her own story makes her the perfect advocate, educator, and influencer for those who are looking for a way out of their own misery.

Her struggles through repeated loss, failing out of college, suicidal thoughts, and a myriad of diagnoses—Tourette Syndrome, epilepsy, bipolar disorder, depression, ADD, OCD, anxiety, alcohol abuse—resonate with people. Olivia overcame all of these obstacles, including speech and language delays, to find her voice as a motivational speaker.

Olivia has a Bachelor of Arts in Interdisciplinary Studies from the University of Central Florida. She also is co-author of *iBRAND, The Next Generation* and partnering workbook *iBRAND: LifePlan*. She launched Staying Sain with her mother, Pam Sain, to help themselves and others navigate profound grief.

She is founder of LGBTQ support group The Butterfly Talks in Orlando, Fla. You can read Olivia's blog at StayingSain.com/blog. For more information, visit **OliviaSain.com**.

Lightning Source UK Ltd.
Milton Keynes UK
UKHW050933010620
364110UK00004B/153